Secret Dance

Poems by

David Stephenson

ISBN: 978-93-6354-966-1

First Edition: 2026
Rs. 200/-

Cyberwit.net
HIG 45 Kaushambi Kunj, Kalindipuram
Allahabad - 211011 (U.P.) India
http://www.cyberwit.net
Tel: +(91) 9415091004
E-mail: info@cyberwit.net

Printed at Repro India Limited.

for Maria Clelia, in case she reads it

You got to have smelt a lot of mule manure before you can sing like a hillbilly.

Hank Williams

Let them cant about decorum, who have character to lose.

Robert Burns, "The Jolly Beggars"

Acknowledgements

I am grateful to the editors of the following publications, where most of these poems first appeared, or were republished:

Autumn Sky Poetry Daily, *Avatar Review*, *Blue Unicorn*, *California Quarterly*, *Extreme Formal Poems*, *Extreme Sonnets II*, *Form in Formless Times*, *The Galway Review*, *The Lyric*, *The Orchards Poetry Journal*, *Plainsongs*, *Poetry Porch*, *Rat's Ass Review*, *The Road Not Taken*, *Shelter of Daylight*, *Ship of Fools*, *Slant*, *Snakeskin*, *Tar River Poetry*, *Valparaiso Poetry Review*, and *Well Met*.

Contents

1. Paper Lanterns

Dawn

Each day opens with a burst of light
when the sun's rays burn through in the east,
as problems shoved in corners for the night
stretch tentacles and strain to be released
and all the world's subsystems turn back on,
supplying tuneless racket everywhere;
familiar worries bask in the new dawn;
a thousand balls jump back into the air.

It's morning in the vale of toil and sin,
the big coin-operated humming hive,
and everything is gathering to begin
another day when you are still alive.
Time to rub the dreams out of your eyes.
The sun is not done shining on you. Rise.

Hold My Beer

One day a great idea just comes you,
like using some old stuff stored in your shed
for some pyrotechnic derring-do,
and you can't get the thought out of your head,
and you're excited but a little scared,
since carrying the stunt out would require
some tricky timing. You feel unprepared
and think of all the ways it could backfire…

And yet key elements are on the scene—
the tires and lumber, and most critically
a full two-gallon can of gasoline—
as if assembled there by destiny.
You know you won't rest till this thing gets done.
Carpe diem. Light the fuse and run.

Wandering Spider

I flick the switch, and watch it cross the floor—
a wolf spider, that has no web or lair
but wanders, an itinerant eyesore,
a little walking knot of legs and hair.

It fishes in the night without a net,
prowling every damp and dark byway,
surviving on a happenstance diet
of unsuspecting creeping, crawling prey;

I too live by my wits, and see it as
a pawn of fortune very much like me,
so I don't step on it, but let it pass
to live its life and seek its destiny

wherever the gap beneath the drywall leads.
I have less empathy for centipedes.

Scar Tissue

They can be beautiful as deserts are,
the little sand-like bands and swirls of skin
encircling the dead heart of a scar,
the patched-up surface where a wound had been.

Run your finger over it. Do you
recall the underlying injury,
or have the details long diffused into
the footnotes of your sprawling history

of small-scale trauma? It's best to forget
the cuts and bruises that no longer hurt
and turn attention to the current set
of jagged edges that you're trying to skirt,

knowing as you face the next ordeal
that all your scars are proof that you can heal.

Chrysalis

One morning, feeling suddenly unwell,
I crawled beneath a twig, as deep within
the first convulsions echoed, and my skin
grew tense and clenched into a stiffened shell,
and I felt all inside me heave and swell,
my parts come loose, my inner joints unpin,
and a coordinated shift begin
to change my basic structure. Time will tell

what kind of brand new animal I'll be
when all is settled and solidified
and I emerge in my transfigured form.
I rarely dare to dream, but hopefully
I'm building something beautiful inside,
not just a slightly different kind of worm.

Tack Hammer

It was my dad's, from way back when;
some thin rod bent into a "U"
with a flared claw on one end
serves as a handle, welded to
a saw-cut piece of thicker rod
shaped with a file, which forms the head;
he must have made it on the job
at the old rail yard repair shed.

He gave it to me when I went
to college, with some more tools in
a hip-roofed box. It's rusted, bent,
objectively ugly as sin,
and yet shines blindingly to me
with beauty only I can see.

One Piece at a Time

It starts with little things you hardly miss,
taken while you look the other way,
and every year there's just a little less,

as when a steady, unobtrusive hiss
continually drains air or steam away.
The little things are easy to dismiss

as you are out attending to business,
focused on collecting your day's pay,
and though you see each year there's less and less

you're confident it can't go on like this,
that someone will step in and save the day
and bring back all the little things you miss—

but you have mis-assessed the whole process,
the things in motion, the advanced decay.
With every year you'll learn to live with less

until you're frog-marched into the abyss,
and as the light fades you'll hear others say
It started with some things we hardly missed
and suddenly we find there's nothing left.

Cement Truck

Turning right out of the cement yard
it arcs into a lurching, creeping roll,
puffing smoke and plainly working hard,
bent beneath the slowly spinning bowl
that stirs the heavy soup of sand and lime
with which it's charged, the contracted payload
it will pour out at the appointed time
into some awaiting form or mold.

Its beauty lies not in its elegance
or subtlety, but in its deft design,
in how tugboat and wheelbarrow elements
are artfully adapted and combined
to raise this glorious ruckus in the street;
not in the abstract, but the concrete.

Detectorist

I take my multi-frequency detector
and closed-back headphones to some likely place—
a park or fairgrounds, any unpaved space
that I can get permission to explore —
and tune the coil for gold, and prospect for
lost rings and jewelry. My unhurried pace
belies the thrill and tension of the chase,
the hope for a long-overdue big score.

I scan the surface layer of dirt and stone
for treasures buried inches underground,
revealed by buzzing sounds in my headphones,
but always also hear faint, ghostly tones
and wonder what strange riches might be found
if I dug deeper, into the unknown.

Dark Matter

...dark matter outweighs visible matter by approximately 5 to 1. Wikipedia

We can't observe it, but believe it's there
from subtle gravitational effects,
from nagging little details that don't square
in how galaxies spin and light deflects;
in fact our calculations indicate
there's much more of it than the visible kind,
a shadow world of enigmatic weight
with which ours is unwittingly entwined.

In most religions, there is interplay
between light and dark forces, thought to be
in balance, with light holding dark at bay,
but studying it scientifically
darkness seems the stronger of the two,
which from human history rings true.

Black Hole

The line through space and time on which you glide
is gradually, irrevocably bent
into a less and less controlled descent
through clouds of glowing dust and gas that hide
a point where darkness has solidified
and space is mangled beyond measurement,
containing light in the entanglement,
so that you can't see through it, or inside,

and as you near it, and begin to feel
your world's geometry degenerate
and everything within you come undone,
if some last window opens to reveal
the plan and purpose of the whims of fate
you won't be able to tell anyone.

Plumber

When fixing plumbing, you are often forced
to bend way down or crawl under a sink,
exposing your gut and/or undershorts,
which is not as funny as people think.

They peek and whisper while you troubleshoot,
and sometimes ask when you're going to be done
and get a pissy little attitude.
The tension builds the longer things go on.

Then when you fix it, everyone's all smiles,
full of sunny, handshaking goodwill,
and they wait nicely with their checkbook while
you laboriously write out the bill

and circle the big fat grand-total fee.
That's a moment with real dignity.

Fortuna

She was the Roman goddess of luck and chance,
wandering around blindfolded all day,
spinning her little wheel of happenstance
to spread good and bad luck along the way.

If there's a local temple, I should go
and light a candle, since I've always been
ridiculously lucky, even though
I'm not the world's most sparkling specimen.

That's what happens when you dish out luck
based on coin flips and dice, casino-style;
good people inevitably get stuck
with endless terrible misfortunes, while

the fair-to-middling prosper and grow old.
Maybe she should take off her blindfold.

2. Labor and Farm

Slaymaker Place

Just down a dirt road from my grandpa's farm,
behind the ruins of a fence and gate,
were an old collapsing house and barn,
locally known as the Slaymaker place,

which didn't mean the people there made sleighs;
"Slaymaker" was the family name of those
who'd farmed it in the horse and reaper days.
I pictured them as gaunt with ragged clothes,

and I was scared and hopeful that I'd see
some Slaymaker ghosts haunting those old shells
but never did. A hired man joked with me,
if you're looking for dead farmers, try hell.

Now their place and my grandpa's are torn down,
with merged and flattened fields where they had been
abiding and awaiting future rounds
of vanity and chasing after wind.

Dog Gauntlet

When I was young, I worked day labor jobs
through a temp agency. Most notably
I joined the team on a dry-fill machine
at a dog food plant. I grabbed the bags
when they were filled and rotated my way
and ran them through a slot to sew them shut.
My other option was a chicken farm.

They put something in dog food so the smell
will make dogs hungry, but make the taste
unpleasant so that dogs don't overeat.
That's the entire theory of dog food.
Since our clothes soaked the smell up, at shift's end
we walked a narrow chain-link tunnel to
the fenced and razor-wired parking lot

while stray dogs from the downwind part of town
came by to prance and bark and growl at us,
attracted by the tantalizing whiffs
that wafted from us as we trudged along,
and also by the lunch meat plant next door.
You're often just a piece of meat at work,
but usually it's not so obvious.

Carhenge

It’s in Nebraska, off the interstate,
up two-lane roads, past irrigation rigs
and railroad and grain elevator towns,
to the remote and alien salt hills
where somebody has spent the cash to build

a replica of Stonehenge with the stones
replaced by junkyard cars all painted gray,
some sunk upright, some welded on the top,
all on a weedy patch of dead flat land
with year-round awful weather. It attracts

art lovers and eccentric druid types,
especially near the winter solstice, though
it’s much too cold to chant out there at dawn.
You’d think locals would dislike the place
for interfering with their wheat farming,

but they’ve set up a small gift shop out front
to sell T-shirts and beer mugs with a smile.
A dollar bill can serve as common ground,
and in this case the juxtaposed vignettes
are maybe more intriguing than the art.

At Sandburg's Grave

It's in a dismal hick town called Galesburg,
noted for patched roofs and lack of paint,
haphazardly laid out and large enough
for points of interest to be hard to find.

Traveling its streets past railroad tracks,
some empty storefronts and a post office
and a scowling grey-haired biker bar,
I found the trail and ended up before

a pair of wood frame buildings with a plaque.
The neighbor lady gave me the fish eye,
and it was clear that no one ever came.
Between the buildings was a good-sized rock,

Remembrance Rock, with ashes underneath,
and looking at it I thought should be
much larger, maybe ten or twelve feet tall,
and carved and painted like a human heart.

Pour Robot

In an aluminum foundry, I saw
a little train of boxes full of sand
running on a rail loop in a pit
that passed beneath an overhead robot
all bundled up in gray asbestos pads

which swiveled between a holding furnace—
where the bucket on its arm was filled
with glowing liquid metal to the brim—
and the pit and rail loop, where it poured
a measured dose into each passing box

as flames and sparks and big billows of smoke
erupted from the vent holes on the top
and cinders hissed and splattered off its pads.
The robot was all scorched and beaten up
like it had been brought back from a world war.

In the forgotten workshops of the past
this task was long performed by human beings
with ladles held between them on long poles,
breathing fire and brimstone, burned and scarred,
and in the shadows, I could see their ghosts.

At Sir George's

My first job was as a busboy at
a restaurant called "Sir George's Royal Buffet"
with waitresses who were older than me
and wore a lot of makeup and perfume.
I was mesmerized and stupefied.

By rule the waitresses shared their tips with me,
and at shift's end, when they all counted up,
they often talked about some customer
who'd been surly and left a measly tip,
shaking their heads and scowling as they spoke

like truck drivers discussing a flat tire,
proposing various stock scenarios
to explain his cheapskate behavior,
spinning entire presumed biographies
featuring a menial, low-paying job

where he gets regularly pushed around
and a humiliating lifelong lack
of romantic success, from puberty on,
before dismissing him as a pitiful.
I've been a big tipper ever since.

Oscar

He was an alcoholic ironworker
employed at a big forge that's now defunct,
and my grandfather on my father's side,
though he was cut off before I was born

due to some drama in an old farmhouse
full of cold-blooded rock-ribbed Methodists
that nobody had much to say about.
I guess they feared his evil influence,

but though I grew up in a bone-dry house
and spent all kinds of time in Sunday school
I've since found a few taverns on my own,
so I guess he's my soulmate, once removed,

and I sometimes try to picture him
when I'm drinking, sitting there with me
with a big drunken grin or sullen scowl,
and in his honor I don't pour one out.

Clown at Gas Station

Last week, at the self-service gas station,
a real orange-haired kid's birthday party clown
emerged from the car right in front of me
and set the hose, and lit a cigarette,
and stood there taking deep drags as it pumped.

Trailing smoke and staring into space,
his painted face looked drawn and beaten down.
There's only so much that a clown can give.
I empathize with all who are employed
And tried to picture what might have gone wrong:

kids getting scared and crying the whole time
or kicking him or stomping on his shoes
or potty accidents or vomiting
or a drunk ex-husband showing up
or any kind of problem getting paid...

At length the pump clunked off. He sorted out
the hose and cap, and took a final drag
on his half-finished smoke, and snuffed it out,
and climbed aboard his rig and drove away,
westward, toward the setting sun. Godspeed.

Outlaws

In a faceless building in Chicago
are racks and racks of laboratory rats
set up for contract medical research,

and the rack-housed rats have lots of rights
backed up by pious federal research rules
guaranteeing their humane treatment

outside of the experiments they're in—
but if they scorn this kindness and escape
and scurry through the basement corridors

they are declared outlaws and lose all rights,
and the exterminators come for them
with trays of poison and spring-loaded traps,

both preferable to the experiments,
the calibrated tortures, for they
don't die in terror, snatched out of a cage.

Herbert Hoover Library

It's right off I-80 in Iowa,
a complex covering several acres like
a golf course, with a clapboard village and

a one-room school house along gravel paths,
but the library is standard brick and glass,
low-slung with a sleek asphalt parking lot;

inside, we learn that Hoover used to be
a top-of-the-line mining engineer,
academic, and administrator

before entering politics to become
the scapegoat Great Depression president,
which is all that people remember now.

Half the scattered cars in the main lot
have out-of-state plates, so Hoover draws
a few tourists, if not whole buses full,

generating local employment
not tied to hog confinements or corn farms,
so he's the default local hero there

and lynchpin of a cottage industry,
although the plaques say he left as a child
and never came back while he was alive.

Payday

My dad's plant was across the railroad tracks
from half a dozen shot and chaser bars,
and on paydays the bars were visited
and stocked with stacks of bills by armored cars,

and women waited at the gates and tracks
at shift changes, to try to intercept
their thirsty husbands in the passing throng
before they cashed and drank up half their check.

At the time, I didn't think about
how desperate those women must have been
to go out on a crowded public street
and chase after their irresponsible men;

I guess I found it droll. But if I'd been
more aware, what could I have done or said?
When people's lives are going off the rails
strangers only frown and shake their heads.

To Whoever Made My Shoes

I think about you when I lace them up,
though I'm not really clear on where you are—
someplace half a world away that's full
of bustling factories and container ships,

and where nobody wears a size twelve shoe.
Are you shocked by our overgrown footwear
and wonder if we're eight or nine feet tall
or have evolved large feet to walk on snow?

Or do you never think of us at all
amid the constant noise, the heat and stench,
the hours of grinding rote activity,
the stress and pressure of the factory?

Ours is a world of ruthless industry
and unavoidable complicity
and I don't know the true cost of my shoes.
I think about you when I lace them up.

Rickie Dale

We never met my father's family,
but after Dad died, my younger brother
searched through records and found his father's grave,
and we decided we should visit it.

The graveyard he was in was a flat field
next to a railroad crossing, with no trees.
Next to the old man's stone was a small one
for Rickie Dale, a son, who had been born

when my father was three, and who had died
just ten years later. He was our uncle,
and his stone was a clue or puzzle piece.
Our older brother's middle name was Dale.

We stood there looking at that chiseled name,
knowing it meant something, just not what,
beyond the normal sorrow of the past.
I looked around at all the other graves,

and thought of all the heartaches they must hold,
and of the secrets I will take to mine.
Then we put a pebble on each stone
and walked away, just as a train rolled by.

3. Winter Wheat

Psalm of David

If you are a little boy
named David on a farm,
there is no better reading than
the sweet, blood-spattered yarn

of your namesake, the shepherd boy
with staff and stones and sling
who killed the giant braggart and
grew up to be a king.

If you skip the religious parts
what's left is super cool,
the only fun thing ever at
the Methodist Sunday School.

But later, reading further on,
assuming there would be
more action, I was shocked to find
that he wrote poetry,

whole pages of it, all church-themed.
The guy broke into song.
Across the centuries between
I wondered what went wrong.

Memory

My memory gets worse as time goes on,
just as the past to be remembered grows,
and having given up on stopping it
I'm working to control what stays or goes,

since every day is like a pane of glass
you crash through, and a thousand pieces fly;
you gather a few handfuls to take home
but most are just abandoned where they lie,

and sometimes how you feel deep down depends
on the specific memories you've kept,
on some uplifting detail you recall
or something that you've managed to forget.

One and Done

When I gaze into the past, I see
a lot of scenes I would play differently
if I had a second chance,

but I play them all cold in one shot,
following or thickening the plot,
unmindful of the aftermath.

My life would be much better with retakes
and strategic deletions of mistakes,
a much-condensed director's cut,

but I'm stuck instead with the raw feed,
the dog's breakfast of muddle and misdeed
daily pouring or petering out,

spinning as it goes a tiresome tale,
poorly paced and full of drab detail,
meandering toward an ending not in doubt.

Canned Chili

The problem with the human brain
is all the thoughts it generates
and cycles through compulsively
for no clear purpose. Thus, while I

observe this slug of foodstuff smoke
and sputter on the stove, I think
about my father, who taught me
the bleak art of preparing it

in the benighted age before
the coming of the microwave.
I ponder some unpleasant math
to estimate what year that was.

I also think of canned food drives
we had for charity at school,
and the assembled sorry piles
of creamed corn and chopped spinach, stuff

I wouldn't choke down for ten bucks.
I hear my fourth grade teacher say
she's sure they're glad for what they get,
and I remember doubting it.

I see the sprawling factory where
my chili's manufactured, full
of vats and troughs and pipes and valves
and clattering machinery

and laborers in overalls
and gas masks moving through the scene,
and stray dogs circling outside
beneath a gray and birdless sky.

And I think glumly of my wife,
away at some grim conference,
all dolled up in her business clothes
and eating fancy hotel food,

and how she'd be appalled to learn
how I'm subsisting while she's gone,
and how I'd better ditch the cans
offsite prior to her return.

I think of all these things at once,
as if the spark plugs in my skull
are firing for the joy of it
or out of boredom. Either way

The moment passes. When I judge
the heated mass *al dente*, I
dump it into a bowl, and crack
a beer open, and eat, and wait

for some new crop of thoughts to seep
into my head and strike me, drawn
like pirates to a keg of rum,
or nuns to church, or sharks to chum.

Night Watch

How would I get by if I lost you?
The question comes to mind unwelcomely
as you're sleeping soundly next to me
and I watch the alarm clock flicker through

its numbers, trying to shoo the thought away,
instead of lying awake pointlessly
contemplating how, specifically,
all we have might fall apart someday,

since for parts of life you just react
to things that happen that you can't control,
to losses that can never be made whole,
and you can't prepare before the fact.

I want to hug you, but you'd get upset
if I woke you up, so I just slide
clumsily over and press against your side.
I doze off, thinking not today, not yet.

Sugar Mountain

Some ants have broken through my kitchen screen
and follow a zigzagging formic path
across unnatural terrain to reach
the sugar bowl, their world's new center-point.

I wonder if they have mythology
explaining it, with ur-ants and whatnot;
if so, I have a prophecy for them
about a scowling, vengeful, bug-spray god—

or I could fix the screen or move the bowl,
avoiding the Old Testament approach.
They're only following their destiny,
like humans, cashing in on a windfall,

and I am wary of inviting Death
onto my property, lest he decide
to bag an extra target while he's here.
So I will fix the screen, and think of them

back in their anthill, telling wide-eyed tales
about the sugar mountain they once found
in an enchanted cave high on a cliff
which like all miracles could never last.

Shelter Cat

for Francesca

Having determined that she needed a cat,
my daughter went to the shelter and brought back
the one next in line to be euthanized,

an older, ornery, ungainly short-hair
that mostly hisses from the bed all day.
It's the unlikely apple of her eye

and rests in feline opulence amid
the fountain and the conical cat cave
and all the overpriced cat toys she buys,

which it takes as its due. It started with
her kind heart melting when she saw its plight.
Nobody who knows her is surprised.

Armored Car

Shall I compare you to an ice cream truck?
You share a common ancestor. Your build
is cubic, a distinct morphology
which marks you both as treasure chests on wheels,

and people gaze upon you as you pass
like children when they hear your cousin's bells,
as if entranced by puppets on TV
or dreaming of the circus or the sea.

B-Team Football Practice

I wore the storied red and white
of Calvin Coolidge Junior High
as a third-string member of
the tackle football team, though I

never appeared in a league game
except for one sad kickoff play
when our side gave up a touchdown.
I went to practice every day

and when the league season was done
they held an extra "B-Team" game
for those who'd rarely played, against
a rival school's reserves. I came

to practice in the freezing cold
the day before. Coach called us "men"
and praised our true love of football
to show up in such weather when

we were only benchwarmers and
no one would come to see us play,
and said we weren't the best athletes
but sure had spirit anyway,

or words to that effect. Inspired,
I asked myself, "Why and I here?"
and ended up skipping the game.
Thus ended my football career.

Window

Last night I saw my father in a dream,
standing in a house I'd never seen,
by a window, working, as in life,
scraping something with a putty knife.

Through the window you could see below
our old home town as it was years ago,
with half-known people acting silent scenes
and everything torn down put back again.

I told him all my troubles and my cares;
he answered while still scraping some spot clear,
saying he never worried about me,
that I'd figure things out eventually.

I woke up feeling rested and serene,
as happy as I can remember being
over what I thought had been revealed,
and then I realized it wasn't real.

Sleepwalk

Time flows like water, ceaselessly,
but also falls like leaves or snow
to coat the shifting world below
with daily layers of debris,

and as I wander, short of cash,
through each successive present day,
on track, in circles, or astray,
I kick up clouds of dust and ash.

Most places I have often been
still harbor ghostly elements
of certain still recalled events
that happened there once way back when,

but if I pause to think about
how things connect and intertwine
and grow and stagnate and decline
I run the risk of zoning out

and sleepwalking through hours or days
obsessing over times long gone
while the ignored world rumbles on,
unfolding while I'm in a haze,

and in the process I forget
to do the chores I need to do
and to devote attention to
the people who are with me yet.

The past should teach, not occupy,
so you can visit, but don't stay,
and only let thoughts drift that way
when you're alone, in case you cry.

Anger Like Acid

Anger like acid eats through everything
hissing as it trails corrosive smoke
and leaving melted stubble in its wake.

Anger like wind arrives in gusts and waves
rattling window panes and slamming doors
and scattering debris along its course.

Anger like liquor gets into your blood
becoming first a habit, then a need,
the gall you drink, the acrid air you breathe.

Anger like a dog stuck in a cage
growls and howls and yanks against its chain
and then gives up, with nothing having changed.

Year's End

Ten years have passed since we stood in the snow
and listened as the preacher someone hired
proclaimed that you were now in paradise.

I figured that she'd never met you once,
but I'm not sure what other choice there'd be
for somebody who didn't go to church.

And the pain has never gone away,
and I think about you every day,
and how I'm living through it and you're not.

And though I tried but never could believe
in heaven, or that anything survives,
I just thought that I should tell you that.

4. This Side of Hell

Rousting Jesus

Hey Chief, wake up. Can you stand up? Let's go.
Christ, what happened to your hands and feet,
and how'd you get those cuts around your head?
Let's have a look. Alright, I guess you'll live.
I don't know what you think you're doing here
but this is a nice, family neighborhood
and there's an ordinance about the park—
it's just for residents, and closed at night.
You need to gather all your stuff and leave.
If you're still here the next time I come through
I'll have to call it in. You don't want that.
Come on, let's go. There's nothing for you here.

On the Road

for Luke

I install industrial robots
in every godforsaken Podunk town
and pole barn plant where our elite sales team
has sold a job through some huge underbid,

so I am front and center to explain
that their job won't be finished by Tuesday
and will cost much more than twelve hundred bucks
and that they need electrical upgrades.

Then I put on my business face and wait
through all the thundering and foot-stomping,
the anger, grief, denial, and bargaining,
the threats to get me fired, the theater

of small-time life, so stale and pitiful.
And through it all I think of all the times
I've been away from home, the things I've missed,
the things I wish were different but which aren't,

and wonder if they really aren't aware
of how the world works at the bottom end
where skinflints cheat each other left and right,
and that sometimes it has to be their turn.

Security Guard

Most people, if they give me any thought,
perhaps assume I didn't qualify
to be a real policeman, and was doomed
to settle for this job to half fulfill
some shattered boyhood dream. Or maybe that
I'm lazy, or a drunk, or otherwise
unsuitable for more rewarding work,
or maybe that I'm simply not too bright.

It's understandable, considering
the get-up that I wear: the bus-boy shirt,
band pants, big-buckled belt, and shiny shoes,
the shoulder patch and Junior G-Man badge.
The whole ensemble has a cop motif.
Put a walkie-talkie in my hand
or stick me with a multitude of keys
and I cannot help looking like an oaf.

I neither chose nor settled for this job;
it simply chanced to be available
when I looked in the want ads years ago.
At another time, I might have been
a dishwasher, or telemarketer,
or cashier at a drug or hardware store.
Fate shook its cup and dumped a load of dice
onto the cosmic felt, and this occurred.

My calling surely has its negatives:
the endless front-desk shifts through which you sit

and sign in visitors—you always get
some jackass who's offended by the drill;
the sudden calls from surly, stressed-out types
who've locked themselves out, and are mad at you;
and now and then the unexpected chance
to hassle with a drunk or lunatic.

And yet it has its pleasures and its charms:
if rude or pompous people come your way,
you have the power to frustrate or annoy
by slowly following elaborate rules;
you also come to know the building's bowels,
the access tunnels, pipe runs, boiler rooms,
and storage spaces buried in its stone,
to which you can discreetly disappear;

and best of all, sometimes you work at night
when everything is empty. Then you move
in silence through deserted offices,
each one with signs of life, a picture here,
a folder there, as if the occupants
had been removed by magic. And you see
how nice it is without them, and you dream
that you're the only person in the world.

Technician

We never call it urine. Rather, it's
the "sample fluid" or the "medium."
A rose by any other name. We get
whole racks of it in erstwhile sterile cups,
brought in from scattered clients drawn to us
by federal law or basic nosiness.
Our labor is to test the stuff for drugs.

The work is stupid-proofed. You pipette drops
of fluid into sections of a tray
with different indicators. If you see
a plus sign, you make a note on the tag.
The hard part is not mixing samples up,
but even that has gotten easier
since they went with the bar codes on the lids.

We have our jokes, like any other job,
bring us another round, this Bud's for you,
the hoary quip about how business stinks,
and stuff you pull on new guys, like the gag
where you get them to ask the boss about
the protocol for floaters in the cup.
It helps to pass the dreary clocked-in hours

without much thought, since thinking doesn't help
in our business. You know that when you get
a positive, and make that little mark,
you're kicking off some distant tragedy.
Somebody's probably going to lose a job

and end up broke, with all that promises
in our indifferent society,

but you don't dare to hint at sympathy
for those poor bastards, or at least their kids,
or ask what difference any of it makes.
That brings a blast of screw-the junkie talk
from your beer buddies, or suspicious looks,
or shrugs and the disquieting response,
if you're so smart, how come you're working here?

That question burrows to the heart of things,
where money rears its powdered, pig-tailed head,
and not the money that the firm collects,
but rather the stark paycheck I accept
which makes me party to it, and my doubts
unseemly. I am in up to my neck.
I'm not the one good pirate on the ship.

But now I'm thinking way too much again.
I doubt the slaves who made the pyramids
debated Pharaoh's building policies;
they stacked their stones and had their cakes and ale.
Their tasks were set by painted courtiers
who sneaked through corridors and whispered deals
in some far capital they'd never see.

Why beat a greasy spot upon the ground
where there was once a dead horse long ago?
Most people cannot change the way things are
or argue themselves happy. This I ought
to understand. I dabble daily with
the nectar of obedience. It is
my lot in life. Bring me another round.

Innkeeper

A Samaritan came in here Tuesday
with a stranger he'd found left for dead
by bandits on the road to Jericho.
He left two gold coins, and said he'd repay
further costs for his upkeep and bed
on his return from where he had to go.

Regrettably, the stranger passed away
and the two coins are spent. If my new friend
indeed returns, I'll do my best to part
more gold from him. I'll probably just say
I had to call some doctor at the end;
any line should work with his soft heart.

Tylenol Killer

I'm the one who doctored headache pills
with cyanide and left them on the shelves
at drugstores. The plan came to me by chance
and kept returning. I became intrigued.
It seemed so simple, and so obvious.

And then I did it, and people did die.
I saw their grieving families on TV,
and that awakened me, the tragedy,
the callousness, the inhumanity.
And no meaning was revealed to me.

I thought I would be caught, and was afraid,
but all of the detectives on the case
got nowhere. It was too senseless to solve.
They worked for months, then gave up one by one.
Now it is buried under later crimes.

I can never tell a living soul.
I would not be forgiven. To confess
would be to face the hatred of the world
alone, to be exposed for all to see.
Redemption is not possible for me.

Others dream and plan. I simply wait.
The past cannot be changed. Someday I'll die,
as faceless as the next guy, and I'll take
my shame and secret with me to the grave,
hoping that there's not an afterlife.

Archaeologist

I specialize in digital remains
from the early space flight period.
At that time most important documents
were stored in myriad ad hoc formats
on primitive distributed networks.
The networks didn't survive through later times,

so all that's left are copies stored off-line
in metal boxes or behind concrete,
encoded optically or magnetically
onto standardized disks or wafers made
of silicon or polycarbonate,
often cached like amulets or coins.

When there is a new find, we classify
its contents by material, size, and shape,
as with arrowheads or pottery.
Then we run through our battery of scans
to see if any can still be accessed,
and in rare cases we recover files.

Most we cannot read, since they are in
machine code for some unknown processor
or an obscure file format long since lost.
And many that we can read are mundane:
hardware manuals, license agreements,
and sales brochures in period boilerplate.

Yet we still sometimes find what we most prize,
a cache of personal or household files
archived in common formats we can read:
financial statements, legal documents,
tax records, letters, wills, and diaries,
and family images and videos.

These assemblages do provide some sense
of everyday life in that remote time,
but much of the material is alien,
describing a callous, superstitious world.
The diaries provide some glimpses of
the inner lives of individuals,

but it's the images and videos
that most evoke a shared humanity.
You see them in small groups, on holidays,
at family gatherings, looking straight at you
and smiling. When you meet them eye to eye
it's poignant, since you know their world is doomed.

Motivational Speaker

I grew up poor, but then most people do.
My dad was not a drunk or anything,
just broke. I still remember ugly scenes
when bill collectors came to chew him out
in front of everyone. He'd come in with
a look that I now recognize as shame.
It was pathetic. But I don't feel I
was traumatized more than the average kid,
considering, though the experience
gave me a lifelong interest in cash.

I've been in the business fifteen years.
I worked the gate for this one guy I knew
from in the service. He had not been much
of a success there, but he sure could work
a country church or small town high school gym.
His pitch was all emotion, rah-rah stuff,
mixed in with Bible verses and football,
but he had contacts, and he got me gigs,
and taught me lots of basic business stuff.
The last I heard he'd started singing hymns.

I use a fairly basic formula.
When I come on, I get someone offstage
to rap a piece of wood next to a mike,
and put my hand up to my ear and say
Do you hear that? That's opportunity.
And then I tell them how I grew up poor,
which, as I said, most people do, or like

to think they did, so that part always sells.
And then I ease into the rah-rah part,
and tell them *You can do it! Dare to dream!*

You have to buy into your pitch yourself,
otherwise it's never going to work.
I truly feel that all I say can help
although sometimes the thought pops in my head
that motivation's not like buying tires,
not something that you pay for at a store,
but something you should generate within,
but there are many others doing this
and whole roomfuls of paying customers,
so it all must be helping somebody.

When I go back to someplace that I've been
a year or two before, I always see
a face or two I recognize. They are
the regulars, who come to hear me say
that they can strike it rich, somehow, someday.
They never do, of course, and yet they keep
attending, and there's no good way for me
to stop them, though I'd like to. I don't need
their money that much, and they make it seem
like I'm just selling false hope, not a dream.

www.ingramcontent.com/pod-product-compliance
Ingram Content Group UK Ltd.
Pitfield, Milton Keynes, MK11 3LW, UK
UKHW041316190726
13845UKWH00025B/315

9 789363 549661